THE STORY OF GEORGE WASHINGTON

A Biography Book for New Readers

Written by
Lisa Trusiani

Illustrated by
John John Bajet

ROCKRIDGE PRESS

To Donna Flanigan,
Elaine Durbach, Maria Concillio,
Rick Parker, Grant Parker,
Grayson Parker
—L.T.

For general information on our other products and services or to obtain technical support, please contact our Customer Care Department within the United States at (866) 744-2665, or outside the United States at (510) 253-0500.

Rockridge Press publishes its books in a variety of electronic and print formats. Some content that appears in print may not be available in electronic books, and vice versa.

Series Designer: Angela Navarra

Interior and Cover Designer: Angela Navarra

Art Producer: Hillary Frileck

Editor: Kristen Depken

Production Editor: Mia Moran

Illustration © John John Bajet; Creative Market/Mia Buono, pp. 3, 12, 21, 27; Charles Willson Peale, p. 54

Illustrator photo courtesy of © Donovan Bajet

ISBN: Print 978-1-64611-115-2 | eBook 978-1-64611-116-9

R0

Printed in China

CONTENTS

CHAPTER 1

A LEADER IS BORN

Meet George Washington

When George Washington was a child, he was tall, strong, and smart, and he liked challenges. He liked to challenge himself in sports and in school. He did hard things until he could do them easily.

When George was a teenager, he gave himself a new challenge. He decided to learn good manners and practice his handwriting at the same time. He read a book about how to be polite. The book had 110 rules, and George copied each one using a quill pen and ink. He wrote the rules carefully. The rules said you should not kill bugs in front of other people, not talk while yawning, and not act happy when your enemy is hurt. Mostly, the rules were about treating other people with respect.

George grew up to have a very important job. It was a great challenge, but George was good at challenges. In 1789, he became the first **president** of the United States of America. No one had been president before because the country was new. If George was a good president, the United States could grow strong. If he was weak or a bully, it might fall apart. George wanted this new country to have a good future.

This is the story of George Washington. Let's take a closer look at who he was and how he helped the United States grow into the country it is today.

George's America

George Washington was born in Virginia in 1732. Today, Virginia is one of 50 states in the United States of America. When George was born, Virginia was a **colony**, one of 13 American colonies. The king of England owned and ruled them. This meant most people in the colonies—including George—were English.

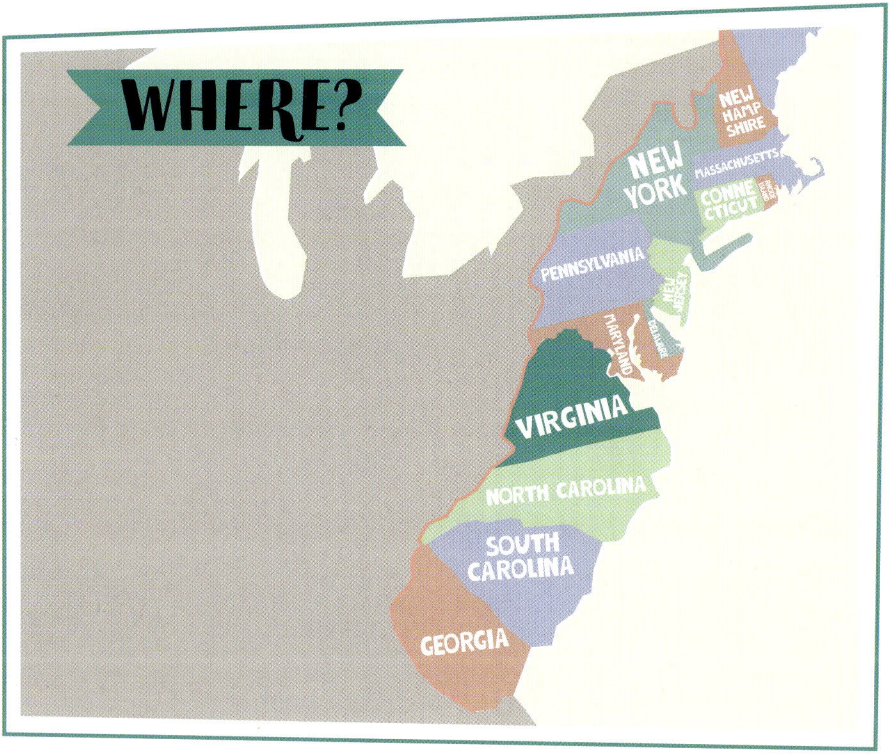

George was the first child born to Gus and Mary Washington. Gus had been married before, but his first wife had died. When Gus met and married Mary, he already had three children. Together, Gus and Mary had six more children. Young George was part of a big family, but he didn't live with his older **half brothers**. They went to school in England.

George's family was rich compared to most families in Virginia. George's father owned farms and thousands of **acres** of land. But the richest families in Virginia owned 100 times more land than the Washingtons!

MYTH & FACT

MYTH: **Colonists** who were born in America stayed in America and never went to England.

FACT: The richest families in Virginia traveled to England for many reasons, including visiting family who lived there.

In Virginia, large farms were called **plantations** and the owner was called a **planter**. The planter lived in a big house with his family. Near the big house were shacks. The people living in these shacks were men, women, and children who were forced to work on the plantation against their will. They were **enslaved** and called **slaves**. They started work before the sun rose and did not stop until after dark. They worked hard, cleaning and cooking for the owner's family and picking crops in the fields. Some were skilled **artisans**. The planters did not pay them for their hard work. None were free because the person who owned the plantation legally owned them. This cruel system was called **slavery**.

Some of the first slaves in the colonies were **Native American**. Over the next 250 years, most slaves were **African**. The first African slaves were kidnapped in Africa, forced onto ships, and taken to the colonies around 1619. More than 100 years later, when George Washington was born, it was still legal to own slaves in all the colonies, even though it was wrong.

Most slaves were in the Southern colonies, including Virginia. In the North, farms were smaller and needed fewer workers. In the South, planters had larger crops like cotton and **tobacco**. As slave owners, they grew rich using the unpaid work of slaves. Some ship captains from the North became rich sailing to Africa and taking the kidnapped men, women, and children to sell to the planters. Slave owners and slave traders believed people who had darker skin were less human than white people from Europe. But many people, mostly in the North, knew slavery was wrong and wanted to make it illegal.

In Virginia, the richest families had ways of staying rich. They became leaders and made laws for the colony. Their sons went to school in England, and some became **officers** in the king's army and **navy**. Their families met at fancy parties. Their sons and daughters married each other. Sometimes their marriages were planned while they were children. Families did this to keep their land together.

The Washington family did this, too: going to school in England, joining the military as officers, and marrying women with land. For hundreds of years in England and in Virginia, George Washington's family was rich and worked at becoming richer.

WHEN?

1657 — George's great-grandfather moves to Virginia.

1674 — George's great-grandfather is given land in Virginia.

1732 — George Washington is born in Virginia.

CHAPTER 2

THE EARLY YEARS

Growing Up in Virginia

George grew up on his family's farms. There were hills, woods, and rivers. George learned to ride horses, hunt, and fish. Sometimes George's father, Gus, worked on the farm, but when he worked at his iron mine, or took extra jobs like being a **tax collector**, George didn't see him for months.

MYTH & FACT

MYTH	FACT
At the age of six, George took a new gift, an ax, and chopped down his father's favorite cherry tree. When his father asked George if he had cut down the tree, George admitted he had.	Years after George died, a man wrote this made-up story about George being honest.

When George was six, he met his older half brother Lawrence for the first time. Lawrence came back from England to manage a farm that belonged to their father. It was later named Mount

Vernon. Gus moved George and the rest of his young family to Ferry Farm, 40 miles away.

Two years later, Lawrence became an officer in the king's navy. He sailed off to war in the **West Indies**. Every letter he sent to George was a treat, and everything about him was exciting. George said Lawrence was his favorite person and someday he would be like Lawrence. When Lawrence came home, George was happy.

Washington Family Tree

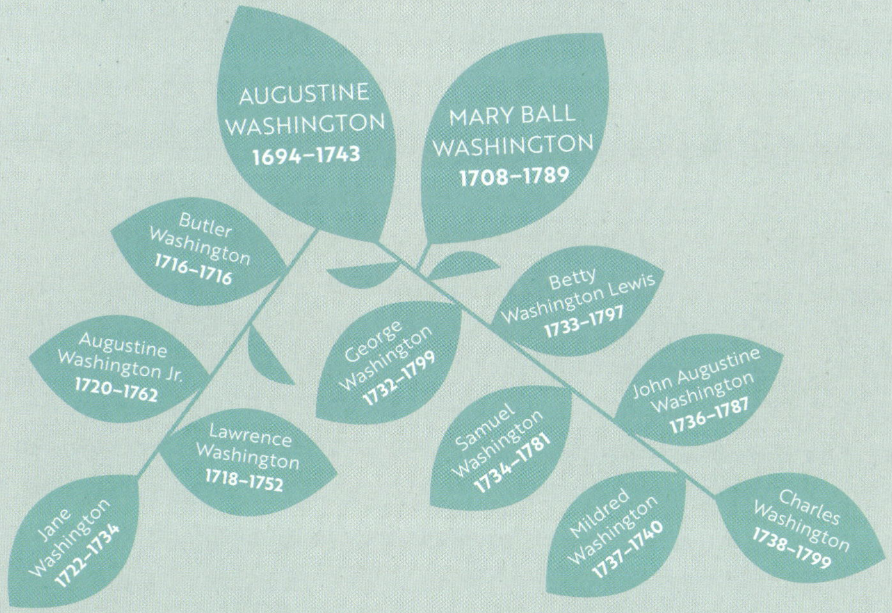

Changes in the Family

George was 11 years old when his father suddenly died. It turned George's life upside down. There wasn't money for George to go to school in England like his older brothers. He had to help his mother run Ferry Farm, and they did not get along. During George's teenage years, he spent more and more time with Lawrence and his wife at Mount Vernon. The more time George spent there, the happier he was.

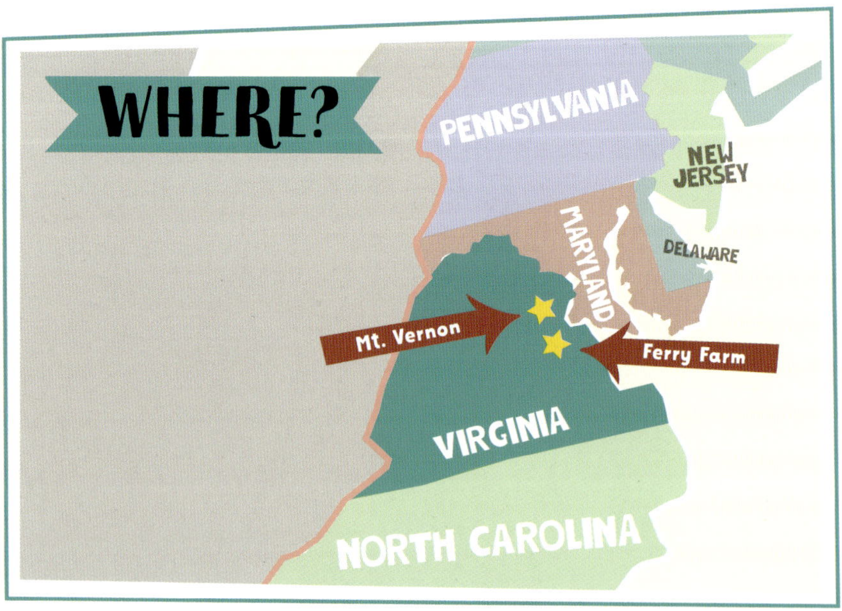

George needed to make money, and Lawrence knew a man who had a job for him. Lord Fairfax owned five million acres of land. He hired George to be a **surveyor** and explore the land. George measured the land and wrote reports about its trees, water, and animals. He told Lord Fairfax about the Native Americans who lived there. George liked working outdoors. He also liked making money and used some to buy his own land.

JUMP IN THE THINK TANK

Do you think US history would be different if George Washington did not take his brother's job in the militia?

Following in His Brother's Footsteps

When George was 20 years old, Lawrence died from an illness. George had loved and admired Lawrence. He asked the king's **governor** in Virginia to give him Lawrence's job. The governor said yes, and George became a major in the Virginia **militia**.

The **French and Indian War** began two years later with England and France fighting about land. Both countries wanted to own the same piece of land west of Virginia. Most of the fighting happened in North America, where French soldiers and French colonists fought English soldiers and English colonists. Tribes of Native Americans joined both sides. George was in the militia and fought for England.

George was brave. At the start of one battle, the officer in charge was shot. Without him, his soldiers lost courage, except for one. As fast as lightning, George rode his horse into the battle.

> "I heard the bullets whistle, and, believe me, there is something charming in the sound."

He shouted for others to join him, as if they were *his* soldiers. He led them to fight bravely.

After five years in the militia, George went home to Mount Vernon. In 1763, England won the war and took control of the land.

WHEN?

- **1743** George's father dies.
- **1748** George first surveys land.
- **1752** Lawrence, George's half brother, dies.
- **1753** George takes Lawrence's military job.
- **1756** England declares war on France.
- **1758** George stops fighting in the war.

CHAPTER 3

MOUNT VERNON

Home Sweet Home

Back at Mount Vernon, George was ready to settle down. He went to a dance, and there, he met Martha Dandridge Custis. George and Martha had a lot in common. They both wanted to live in the country. They both liked visits with friends. They both wanted to have a family. In fact, Martha already had two children. She had been married before, but her first husband had died. Martha also had valuable land and more than 100 slaves. George and Martha were married in 1759.

Plantation Farming

By the age of 29, George not only lived at Mount Vernon, he owned it. George **inherited** Mount Vernon after Lawrence died. For George and Martha, Mount Vernon was their home, but it was also a business. George had to decide many important things about his farm, like what to grow. At first, he grew tobacco to sell in England. He made good money until the price of tobacco went down. Then he and all the other Virginia planters made less money.

George tried growing other crops. He grew more than 50 kinds of plants to find the ones that could make the most money. He finally decided on **wheat**, and he built a machine to remove the wheat grain from the rest of the plant so it could be turned into flour. People

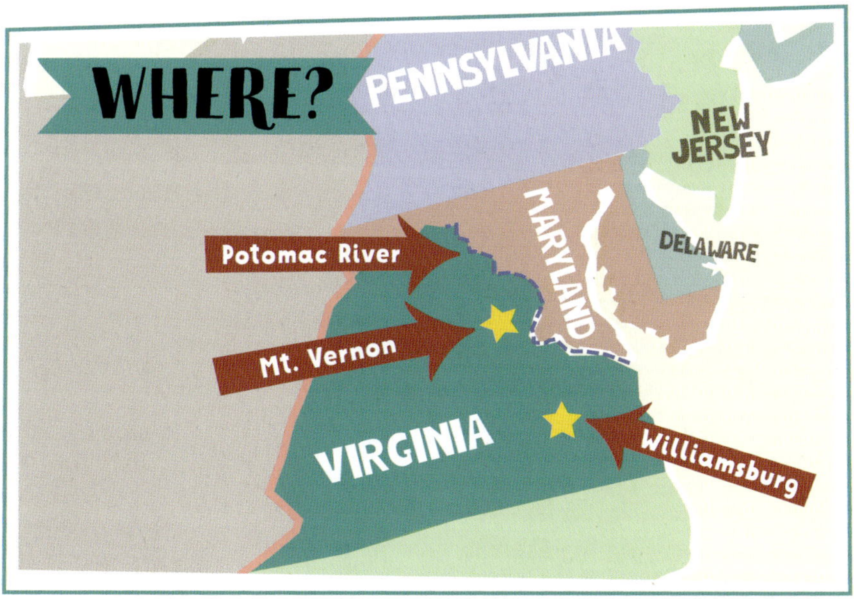

bought the flour to make bread. George also grew other grains like **rye**. He used a machine to turn the rye into **whiskey** for adults to drink. His whiskey business made money. It became famous across all the colonies.

Mount Vernon was on a big river called the **Potomac**. The river was another way for George to make money. He sent slaves out in boats, and they fished with nets. They caught tons of fish, to eat at Mount Vernon and for George to sell near and far. It took time, but George and Martha, and hundreds of slaves, changed Mount Vernon from a tobacco farm to a business with three major products: wheat, whiskey, and fish.

George wanted Mount Vernon to grow. He had enslaved people build more rooms onto his house, making it a mansion. There was now a blacksmith's shop where slaves made tools, and a carpentry shop where slaves made boxes, boats, and furniture. There was a factory where slaves prepared fish to be sold. There was the flour mill, and the whiskey-making building. George owned all of it, including the people, who were given two sets of clothes per year and just enough food to keep them healthy enough to work.

George did not spend all his time at Mount Vernon. He often took trips to a nearby city called Williamsburg. The **government** of Virginia was there. Men who owned land could **vote** for leaders to **represent** them and make laws for the colony. They voted for George. The group of

representatives that included George was called the **House of Burgesses**. George helped make laws for 15 years and enjoyed his work. Then things began to change.

WHEN?

George is elected to the House of Burgesses.	**1758**
George marries Martha Dandridge Custis.	**1759**
George becomes the owner of Mount Vernon.	**1761**
George sells whiskey, wheat, and fish instead of tobacco.	**1766**

CHAPTER 4

BREAKING AWAY FROM ENGLAND

The Boston Tea Party

George had been **elected** to the House of Burgesses, a group that represented colonists in Virginia. But colonists could not elect anyone to represent them in England, where many laws were made. They thought it was unfair to pay taxes, or extra charges, to England if they had no one to represent them in England. Every time England put a tax on things the colonists bought, the colonists became angrier. Their anger boiled over when England put a tax on tea.

George Washington didn't want to pay a tax on tea. He stopped drinking tea, and drank coffee instead.

One night, three English ships were in Boston Harbor in Massachusetts, another colony, with tea from China. More than 100 colonists climbed aboard the ships. They broke open hundreds of wooden boxes filled with the dried tea and dumped it into the water. Today, this **protest** is called the Boston Tea Party. In George's day, it was called Destruction of the Tea.

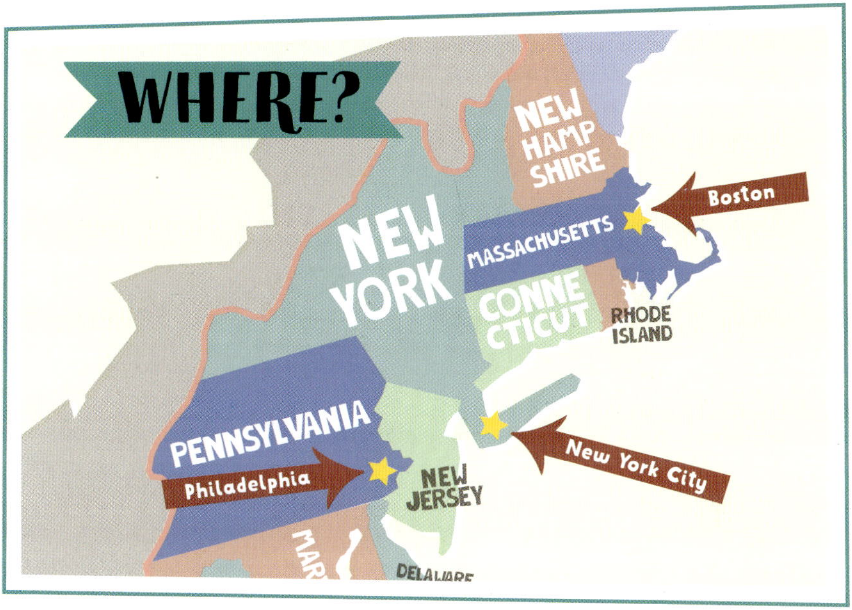

A Declaration Is Made

England wanted to punish the colonists in Boston. The king sent his soldiers to shut down Boston Harbor. No ships went in. No ships went out. No goods to buy or sell could come through the harbor. England would keep it shut until the colonists paid for all the ruined tea. The colonists refused.

George and the other leaders of Virginia took Boston's side. On June 1, people in Virginia

JUMP IN THE THINK TANK

Do you think some people who protested in Boston or Virginia were afraid? How do you think it is possible to protest even when you are afraid?

refused to go to work. This was a protest. They were protesting England shutting down Boston Harbor. To punish Virginia for this protest, England shut down the House of Burgesses. George and other members of the House met in small groups to decide how to handle England. Leaders in the other colonies did the same.

In 1776, George traveled to Philadelphia, Pennsylvania, for a meeting called the **Second Continental Congress**. Here, representatives from all 13 colonies met to create a new country. They wrote a document called the **Declaration of Independence**. It stated that the colonies were

> "Liberty, when it begins to take root, is a plant of rapid growth."

no longer part of England. They were a new country: the United States of America.

George and the other leaders knew that England would not agree to let the colonies go. They sent the declaration to the king and prepared for war.

Representatives at the Second Continental Congress asked George Washington to lead the new country's army. George stopped to think. He wasn't sure he would be a good leader. In the French and Indian War, he had not led

MYTH & FACT

MYTH: George Washington had wooden teeth.

FACT: George had terrible problems with his teeth, and dentists back then did not know as much as they do now. George wore **dentures**, or false teeth, but none were made of wood. They were made of **ivory** and other materials.

thousands of men. And he had been young then. Now his red hair was white, and his teeth were all gone except for one. George worried that he was too old.

Could he win a war against England, the most powerful country in the world? George Washington said yes, and agreed to lead the **Continental Army**. His new country needed him.

WHEN?

Colonists protest unfair taxes with the Boston Tea Party. **1773**

England shuts down the House of Burgesses. **1774**

The Declaration of Independence is written and adopted. **1776**

George becomes the leader of the Continental Army. **1776**

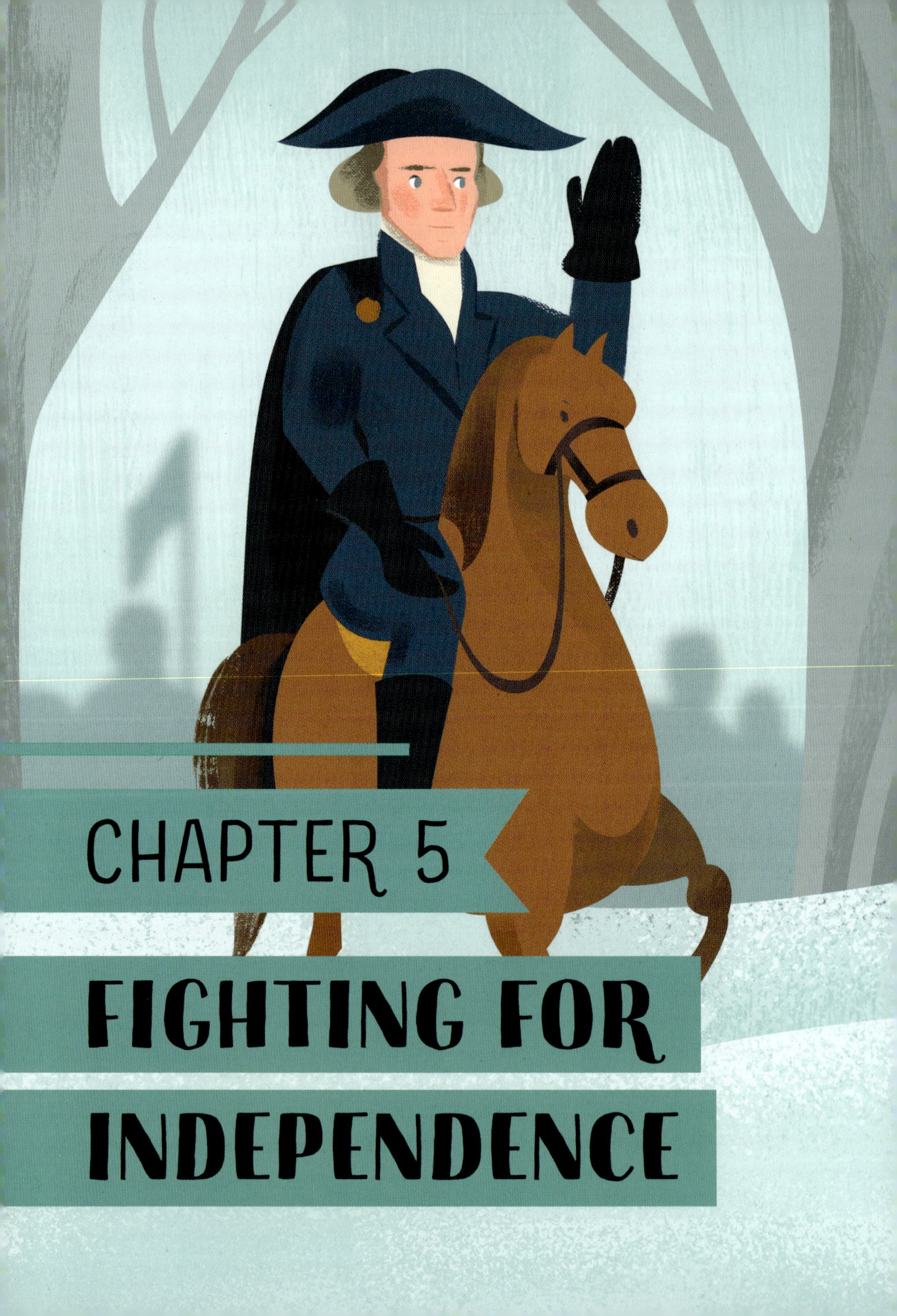

CHAPTER 5
FIGHTING FOR INDEPENDENCE

Gathering the Army

As the **commander in chief** of the Continental Army, George Washington was now in charge of leading the United States in the **Revolutionary War** against England. But his troops were no match for England's army, which had more soldiers and more supplies. George needed thousands of men to join. He asked the states to **draft**, or force, men to join the army.

Of course, having thousands of men was not enough. He needed his soldiers to be trained. They were young. They hadn't fought before. George asked a German officer, Baron von Steuben, to train the soldiers. The baron showed them how to work together. They practiced until everyone moved the same way at the same time.

George also turned to other countries for help. France was happy to help fight its old enemy, England. From the beginning of the war, France sent blankets, clothing, cannons, and other

> Discipline is the soul of an army.

supplies. But George needed more, so France sent its soldiers and its navy.

George was not like other generals, who made battle plans but watched the fighting from far away. George bravely led his soldiers into battles. He fought alongside them across the states. Most of the war was fought in New Jersey, New York, and South Carolina. Some battles had more than 25,000 soldiers fighting one another.

MYTH & FACT

MYTH: Like George, all colonists were **Patriots**—people who wanted to win the Revolutionary War and be independent from England.

FACT: Some colonists were **Tories**, meaning they were loyal to the king. At least 15 percent of colonists were loyal to England. Some fought for England and against George Washington.

Long Winters

Every year, fighting stopped during winter. It was too cold. There was too much snow. One terrible winter, the Continental Army stayed in a village called Valley Forge in Pennsylvania.

George was happy when his wife, Martha, joined him. Many soldiers had their wives and children with them when they were away from the battlefields.

At Valley Forge, George worried about his soldiers. They were called a **ragtag** army because their clothes had turned to rags. They did not have warm clothing. Many had no shoes, and George saw that their bare feet bled as they walked through ice and snow. They had little food. George was very upset that farmers nearby had grown enough food but some wouldn't sell it to the American soldiers. They sold it to the English instead, because the English soldiers could pay more.

JUMP IN THE THINK TANK

George Washington trusted Benedict Arnold. He was a Patriot and an officer, who won a big battle for the Continental Army. Then Benedict sold military secrets to the English for a lot of money. Someone who switches sides like this is called a **traitor**. Why do you think some people become traitors?

George was a strong leader. But without proper food, clothing, and other supplies, his army grew weak. Many soldiers died. Even with help from France, Spain, and the Netherlands, the United States was struggling. George feared his army would lose the war.

WHEN?

- **1776** — The Revolutionary War begins.
- **1777** — George and his army spend the winter at Valley Forge.
- **1780** — Benedict Arnold becomes a traitor.

CHAPTER 6

VICTORY!

A Winning Battle

In 1781, George knew thousands of tired English soldiers were camped in Yorktown, Virginia. It was a good moment to attack Yorktown, but George was far from Virginia and needed more soldiers to win a battle.

Then he learned that French ships carrying thousands of French soldiers were sailing to Yorktown. They wanted to help the Americans win a battle. George quickly led his men south to Virginia.

For three weeks, George and his troops fought the English soldiers. The French navy **bombarded** them. On October 19, the English general surrendered. George had won the Battle of Yorktown.

After the Continental Army won two more big battles in the next two years, the United States of America and England signed a peace **treaty**. The Revolutionary War was over.

George Washington and his army had won independence for the United States.

George had been commander in chief of the Continental Army for eight years—the entire war. In 1783, he retired from the army. He was a hero. He was very happy to go home to Mount Vernon to be with Martha and their family.

MYTH & FACT

MYTH: George Washington wore a wig.

FACT: It was fashionable for gentlemen to have white hair. Many wore wigs, but George powdered his real hair to make it look white.

More Work to Be Done

Once George was home, he worried about the new country. Before the war, George and the other leaders met in Philadelphia and wrote instructions for governing the United States. But now the states weren't following the rules. They made their own money. They made their own deals with foreign countries. They made their own armies. George knew the country would fall apart if the states didn't work together.

In 1787, George and the other representatives from all the states held a meeting called the **Constitutional Convention** in Philadelphia, Pennsylvania. They made decisions about setting up the country and how it would rule itself. They wrote the instructions and rules in a document called the **Constitution**.

The Constitution says all the states are represented in a **federal** government made of three parts: **Congress**, the president, and the **courts**. Congress makes laws, the president enforces the laws, and the courts explain the laws. All three parts have equal power.

JUMP IN THE THINK TANK

Why do you think it was a problem for states to act like separate countries? What could George have been worried about?

"The basis of our political system is the right of the people to make and to alter their constitutions of government."

Now it was time for the representatives to find a president, a leader who could unite the country. When people suggested George, he said he didn't want to be president. He wanted to stay home at Mount Vernon. George agreed to be president if he received the most votes. The representatives voted, and George won easily. He became president. John Adams had the next highest number of votes, so he became **vice president**. George promised to do his best for his country.

WHEN?

George, with help from France, wins the Battle of Yorktown. **1781**

The Revolutionary War ends. **1783**

The Constitutional Convention begins. **1787**

George is elected as the first president of the United States. **1789**

CHAPTER 7

THE FIRST PRESIDENT

A New Start

George Washington became president in 1789. He went to New York City—the country's **capital** at the time. He stood before a crowd and said the oath of office: "I do solemnly swear (or affirm) that I will faithfully execute the office of President of the United States, and will to the best of my ability, preserve, protect, and defend the Constitution of the United States." Those are the exact words written in the Constitution, and the exact words he said.

As president, George was careful to follow the rules of the Constitution. He had to decide many things. He had to decide how the United States should act in the world.

George put together a group of advisers, called his **cabinet**. They gave him advice, and he listened to their ideas. It made George unhappy when they argued with one another, but he listened anyway.

Some countries wanted the United States to help them. For example, France and England had started fighting again, and France asked the United States to help by sending troops. George listened to the people in his cabinet and decided

not to help France or England. Not picking sides meant the United States was **neutral**. George believed that, as a new country, the United States was not strong enough to help a country at war.

President Again

George Washington was elected president twice in a row. Each time, he was president for four years. For the eight years that he was president, there was peace.

While George was president, the country had to decide where its new capital would be. Since George had been a surveyor when he was young, he knew about land. He helped pick the spot, right on the border of Virginia and Maryland. He helped design the city and the **White House**.

> "The Constitution vests the power of declaring war in Congress."

All future American presidents would live there, even though George never did himself.

What should this new city—the home of the federal government—be called?

JUMP IN THE THINK TANK

Do you think being the commander of the army made George Washington a better president?

The representatives in Congress voted to name the capital of the United States after George, so they called it Washington. They wanted to honor George for winning the Revolutionary War, and for being the country's first president.

Many people wanted George to be president a third time. But George didn't want future presidents to act like kings, or to stay in office too long. He believed it was very important for each president to hand over power peacefully to the next president. So he said no to a third term and went home to Mount Vernon.

George still thought carefully about the future of the country. His feelings about slavery were different than before the war. Now George believed slavery was wrong. He also believed it would divide the country someday.

In his will, George gave instructions for the 124 enslaved people he owned to be freed. A few years after returning to Mount Vernon, George got sick, and he died at the age of 67.

George Washington is called the "father of his country" because he did so much to shape the United States of America into the nation it is today.

WHEN?

George is elected president for a second term.

1793

George returns to Mount Vernon.

1797

George dies at Mount Vernon.

1799

CHAPTER 8

SO . . . WHO WAS GEORGE WASHINGTON ?

Challenge Accepted!

George Washington helped create a new country, the United States of America. Let's test your knowledge of George Washington and his **legacy** in a who, what, when, where, why, and how quiz.

1 Where was George Washington born?

- A Virginia, an American colony in the South
- B Massachusetts, an American colony in the North
- C England
- D France

2 What war did George Washington fight in as a young man?

- A The French and Indian War
- B The Horse and Buggy War
- C The Chicken and Egg War
- D All of the above

3 What did George Washington produce at Mount Vernon that he sold to make money?

- A Wheat
- B Fish
- C Tobacco
- D All of the above

4 **What country ruled the 13 colonies?**

→ A Denmark
→ B England
→ C Italy
→ D Brazil

5 **What important document announced that England no longer owned and ruled the American colonies?**

→ A The Gettysburg Address
→ B The Articles of Impeachment
→ C The Declaration of Independence
→ D The Presidential Declaration

6 **Which country or countries helped the colonists fight England during the Revolutionary War?**

→ A France
→ B Spain
→ C The Netherlands
→ D All of the above

7 **What job did George Washington have?**

→ A Housepainter
→ B Shipbuilder
→ C President of the United States
→ D Schoolteacher

8 **Why didn't George Washington live in the White House?**

→ A There wasn't a barn for his horses

→ B He was president before it was built

→ C It was painted purple, not white

→ D All of the above

9 **Did President George Washington act like a king?**

→ A No, Congress and the courts had power equal to his

→ B No, he wasn't born president, he was voted in

→ C No, he did not wear a crown

→ D All of the above

10 **Why is George Washington considered a hero?**

→ A He was commander in chief of all Revolutionary War forces on the United States side

→ B He won the Revolutionary War with his troops, even without proper food, clothing, and weapons

→ C He was the first president of the United States, and he used the Constitution to do a good job

→ D All of the above

ANSWERS: 1. A; 2. A; 3. D; 4. B; 5. C; 6. D; 7. C; 8. B; 9. D; 10. D

Our World

The United States of America has lasted for nearly 250 years. When George Washington became president, many people around the world thought the United States would fail. They thought, how can a country get by without a king? Who will tell people what to do?

When George was president, he didn't want to act like a king. He wanted everyone to follow the instructions in the Constitution—and to this day, we still do. Look around. Do you see TV shows or newspapers not made by the government? That's freedom of the press. Do you have churches, synagogues, or mosques in your city or town? Do you know people who do not believe in a religion or a god? That's freedom of religion. Are you allowed to say that you disagree with the president? That's freedom of speech.

These **freedoms** are in the Constitution. Other freedoms and **rights** are, too. George Washington did not become president to use those freedoms for himself. He kept them strong for "all men," as it is written in the Declaration of Independence. Today, "all men" doesn't only mean white men who own land, as it did in George's time. It includes people who don't own land, and all men and women of all races who live in the United States of America.

George was the first president. He used the Constitution as an instruction book for building the new government. It was not always clear what the words in the Constitution meant. George, along with the other **Founding Fathers**, Congress, and the courts, took the ideas in the Constitution and made them work in the real world. George Washington is called the father of his country because he did so much to shape the new country's future.

JUMP IN THE THINK TANK FOR MORE!

Now let's think a little more about what George Washington did, why he did it, and the ways he changed our world.

→ Why did George believe the Constitution was more important than his own presidency?

→ The words "all men are created equal" are in the Declaration of Independence, written in 1776. What do you think "all men" means? Has the meaning changed over time?

→ What do you think is worth fighting a war for?

→ All presidents after George Washington have followed in his footsteps. What does this mean? If someone is following in your footsteps, what can you do to lead them in the right direction?

Glossary

acre: A measurement of land. One acre is 43,560 square feet of land. The word for more than one acre is **acres**.

African: Having to do with the continent of Africa

artisans: People who are skilled at making things by hand

bombard: To attack with bombs or heavy gunfire. To bombard in the past is **bombarded**.

cabinet: The group of top government officials who advise the president of the United States

capital: The city where the government of a country or region is located

colony: Land that is owned by a country, usually a country that is far away. People who live in a colony are **colonists**. The word for more than one colony is **colonies**.

commander in chief: The top leader of a country's military

Congress: The group of elected people who make the laws for the United States

Constitution: The document written right after the United States became a country that lays out basic laws, instructions, and rules for how the United States must be run

Constitutional Convention: A meeting in 1787 where powerful American leaders wrote the United States Constitution

Continental Army: The army of American colonists who fought against the English army in the Revolutionary War

courts: One of the three parts of the federal government in the United States. They decide how laws should be followed.

Declaration of Independence: The 1776 document announcing the American colonies were a separate country, no longer part of England

dentures: A set of teeth that are not real, but are made to work and look like real teeth

discipline: The ability to obey orders

draft: To force someone to join the military

elect: To pick someone by voting. The process is called an **election**, and the winner is **elected**.

enslaved: Forced to 1) work for no pay, 2) obey, and 3) give up freedom

federal: Having to do with the central or national government of the United States. This is different from the government of each individual state.

Founding Fathers: The group of American leaders who united the 13 colonies, led them in their fight for independence from England, and helped establish a government for their new country

freedom: The ability to think, speak, and behave as you want without restrictions

French and Indian War: A war from 1754 to 1763 in which England fought France for control of land in America

government: A system of rules and people that manage a city, state, or country

governor: Leader of a state government or colony

half brothers: Brothers with only one parent that is the same. In other words, two brothers who have the same mother but different fathers, or the same father but different mothers.

House of Burgesses: A group of people voted into government to make and change laws in the colony of Virginia. The House was created in 1619 and ended in 1776.

inherit: To get something as a gift from a person when he or she dies

ivory: Material that makes up the tusks of animals, like elephants

legacy: A gift from someone who has died. The gift can be physical or non-physical, like ideas, information, or a system.

liberty: Freedom

militia: People with some military training ready for emergency service. Not part of a country's army.

Native American: A member of the group of people who lived in America before Europeans arrived, or a descendant of those people

navy: The branch of a country's military that has ships and operates mainly at sea

neutral: Not taking sides in a conflict

officer: A person in the military with authority and a formal title

patriot: A person who loves and is loyal to his or her country. In the Revolutionary War, Americans who wanted George Washington's army to win were called Patriots.

plantation: A large farm that grows crops to be sold, like cotton and tobacco

planter: The manager or owner of a plantation

Potomac: A river passing through Maryland; Virginia; Pennsylvania; Washington, DC; and West Virginia

president: The elected leader of the United States of America. Some other countries also elect a president.

protest: An action to show you disagree with something

ragtag: Worn, ragged, tattered, faded, poor

represent: To speak or act for someone officially. A person who speaks or acts for someone in an official way is a **representative**. For example, the voters in the colony of Virginia elected representatives to go to the House of Burgesses.

Revolutionary War: A war from 1775 to 1783 that led to America's independence from England

rights: Legal permission to have certain freedoms or act in certain ways

rye: A grain that can be used to make flour for bread, and some alcoholic drinks, such as whiskey, vodka, and beer

Second Continental Congress: The American colonies' chosen government from 1775 to 1781

slavery: A system in which people are forced to 1) work for no pay, 2) obey, and 3) give up freedom

slaves: People forced to 1) work for no pay, 2) obey, and 3) give up freedom

surveyor: A person who measures, explores, and writes a report on a piece of land

tax: Money that a government makes people pay

tobacco: A plant that is chewed or smoked using a pipe, cigar, or cigarette

Tories: Americans who wanted England to win the Revolutionary War. If there is only one, he or she is a **Tory**.

traitor: A person who acts against his or her country

treaty: An agreement between countries

vice president: The president's second-in-command, who will take over if the president can't lead anymore

vote: To decide on something or someone officially

West Indies: A geographic area that includes Cuba, Jamaica, Haiti, Puerto Rico, and many other islands. It's also called the Caribbean.

wheat: A grain that can be used to make flour for bread

whiskey: An alcoholic drink made from a grain, such as rye or barley

White House: The official home of every United States president since 1800

Bibliography

American Battlefield Trust. www.battlefields.org.

Ferling, John. "Myths of the American Revolution." *Smithsonian Magazine*. January 2010. www.smithsonianmag.com/history/myths-of-the-american-revolution-10941835/.

Friends of Little Hunting Creek. Accessed September 19, 2019. http://www.friendsoflittlehuntingcreek.org/description/history.htm.

George Washington's Mount Vernon. Accessed September 10–21, 2019. www.mountvernon.org/.

Grogg, Robert. "Where Oh Where Should the Capital Be?" *White House History*, no. 34 (Fall 2013). www.whitehousehistory.org/.

Kelly, Kate. "George Washington (1732–1799): Childhood and Early Years." America Comes Alive. Accessed October 8, 2019. https://americacomesalive.com/.

Khan Academy. "US History, Road to Revolution (1754–1800)." Accessed September 17, 2019. www.khanacademy.org/humanitities/us-history/road-to-revolution/.

Knott, Stephen. "George Washington: Foreign Affairs." "George Washington: The American Franchise." University of Virginia, Miller Center. Accessed October 9, 2019. https://millercenter.org.

Library of Congress. "George Washington's First Inaugural Address, 30 April 1789." www.loc.gov/.

National Park Service. "George Washington Birthplace National Monument Park." Last updated July 26, 2019. www.nps.gov/gewa/index.htm/.

Tillson, Albert H., Jr. "Gentry in Colonial Virginia." *Encyclopedia Virginia*. Virginia Foundation for the Humanities. Last modified December 6, 2012. https://www.encyclopediavirginia.org/Gentry_in_Colonial_Virginia.

Washington, George. *George Washington Papers, Series 5, 1767–1775*. Retrieved from Library of Congress.

Acknowledgments

I am grateful both to George Washington, for being loyal to the US Constitution as he shaped the office of the presidency, and to the men and women since then who have worked to maintain the integrity of our constitutional systems and principles. Much work remains.

There are many individuals to thank personally for supporting and encouraging my writing of this book as well as other projects. Topping the list are my husband, Rick Parker, and our children, Grant and Grayson; my sister, Donna Flanigan; and my friends Elaine Durbach and Maria Concillio. They have been generous, loving, and kind.

I wish to thank my editors, I.K., L.B., K.D., M.C., S.J., H.M., and F.N.; my current book group: Donna Flanigan, Jennifer Stone Meserve, Peggy Pisini, Suzanne Connolly, Susan Blethen, Sarah A. Verville, Marna Miller, and Paula Watson; and author Jim Murphy, who gave me important advice early in my career. I'd also like to thank my friends and family who have offered important support, often outside the sphere of writing: Sean, Connor and Joseph Flanigan, Mike Robinson, Linne Stuckey, Peggy Excell, Marshall Norstein, Jonathan Glasser, Irene Kelly, Megan Howard, Jess Esch, Laura Hitchcock, Rick Guinee, Pete Bickmore, Gale Connor, Michael Fortier, Liz Ventre, Beth Mattson, Sheryl Wung, Russell Christian, Danni Mersky, Mark Chiarello, Nina Kitabayashi, Lynn Martin, Jamie Buckley, Patti Estes, Patrick Connolly, Julie Baither, Paulo Pacheco, Cathy Stratton, Jane Alessandrini Ward, Marisa Lori and her parents and grandmother, Maria, Robin Locke Monda and Bobby Monda, George and Nancy Miller, Susan Neufeld Trusiani, Miriam Sumner, Angelo DeCesare, Eliot Brown, Arlene Puentes, Brad Stone, Larry Shell, Tina Benson, Michael Vos, Cindy Zimpfer, Heidi Gensch, Rusty Trier, the Joyce Families, Gale Connor, Sid Jacobsen, and Lia Brown. Always and forever, I thank my parents, Annamarie Ross Trusiani and Paul J. Trusiani.

— L.T.

About the Author

LISA TRUSIANI is a versatile and award-winning author who is happiest writing for children and teens. She loves when her work involves researching the past, and asking, "Who, what, when, where, and why?" She often imagines going back in time to meet trailblazers and other fascinating people. Lisa has written hundreds of stories and activities for Marvel Entertainment, DC Comics, Disney, Golden Books, and King Features Syndicate, as well as traditional book publishers and educational publishers. Her work has received the iParenting HOT Media Award, National Parenting Center Seal of Approval, NAPPA Gold Award, and several Parents' Choice Awards. She was also a winner of the Staples Invention Quest, and she wrote the music for an award-winning documentary about the New York City subway. Lisa treasures time spent with family and close friends.

About the Illustrator

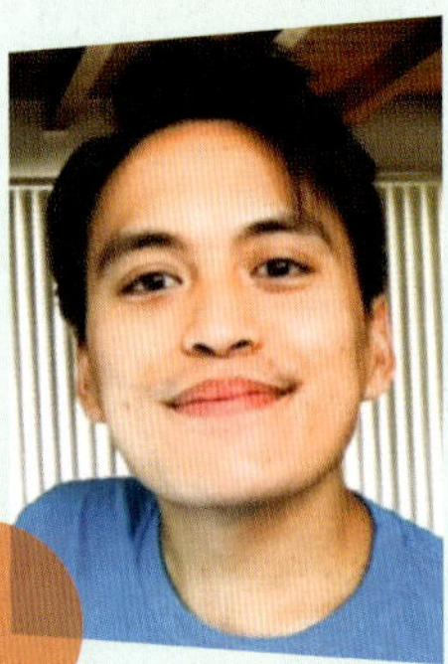

JOHN JOHN BAJET is a Los Angeles–based visual development artist working in animation and picture books. He has worked as a prop designer and color stylist in animation for *The Tom and Jerry Show*, as well as the PBS digital web series, *Biggest Bravest Brother*. Past clients include Hasbro, Scholastic, PI Kids Publishing, and Cottage Door Press. For more info please visit **johnbajet.com**.